Twenty-Five Words Toward the Truth

#25wtT

SKIP MASELLI

authorHOUSE®

AuthorHouse™
1663 Liberty Drive
Bloomington, IN 47403
www.authorhouse.com
Phone: 1 (800) 839-8640

Published by AuthorHouse   03/10/2016

ISBN: 978-1-5049-6857-7 (sc)
ISBN: 978-1-5049-6858-4 (e)

Library of Congress Control Number: 2016903914

Print information available on the last page.

Any people depicted in stock imagery provided by Thinkstock are models,
and such images are being used for illustrative purposes only.
Certain stock imagery © Thinkstock.

This book is printed on acid-free paper.

Contents

For my grandfather, Edward Heller; a man who
claimed no religion, but was truly a man of God.
He opened my mind.

And for my mother Susan Maselli, Edward's daughter,
without whom there'd be no container nor content.
She opened my heart.

Preface

Why Twenty-Five Words toward the Truth: #25wtT?

There is a saying in Russian, "*Kratkost sestra talanta*," which appropriately has no direct translation, but generally means, "In order to share some wisdom, sayings do not have to be extensive." My hope is that *#25wtT* stimulates conversation and deep listening—or *sobhet* as the Turkish say—among my readers. These sayings are intended to simmer within and tantalize the mind to step into the space of the heart, as well as inspire the heart to disclose itself within the realm of the mind. The journey in between the heart and mind, well, that awaits *your own touch*. May you write of your own heart what you read in mine.

The idea for *#25wtT* began when I noticed that many of my shorter poems and brief phrases contained in the longer poems were getting particular attention from readers. I surmised that some just prefer to read short things on which they can reflect, repost, or tweet. Each seems to tug at the imagination and musing of my friends, generating questions and speculations as to what these short passages mean. Perhaps the Russian proverb is correct, that the meaning of a poem is inversely proportional to its length.

To my delight, many of these poemettes turned out to be exactly twenty-five words, and through their meaning and metaphor, I started calling them, *Twenty-Five Words toward Truth*. Since their length made them easier to tweet, I added the hashtag and abbreviation, thus becoming *#25wtT*.

I was pondering this quote attributed to Mevlana Celaleddin-i Rumi: "The nature of reality is this: It is hidden, and it is hidden, and it is hidden."

And I thought about the introduction to this book. The meaning of these poemettes is hidden from you, by you, and within you. We take for granted that reality is something as "apparent and same" to everyone. But the truth of reality is not to be confused with the *reality of truth*; in the former, truth is both hidden and there, and in the latter expression, it is *hidden there*. The power of unfound truths spins the universe. It is the amazing and humbling void of the *true* truth's absence that compels the spirituality initiated to fill it. It is this absence that stirs us to seek its meaning within the external world of poetry, beauty, movement, romance, and esotericism. What unites the world for all of us is not the distribution of riches, but the revelation of wealth within our individual poverty—*faqr fakhri (Arabic)*. What every poemette in *Twenty-Five Words toward the Truth* fails to reveal in its brevity can be endlessly expounded upon within the unfathomable nothingness inside us.

In keeping with the twenty-five-word spirit, here are some bullets on what #25wtT is about. Each is twenty-five words—count them:

- A collection of twenty-five-word poemettes that were inspired by something longer. Consider them simply as velveteen petals fallen from the rose, clipped from the thorns.

- Sometimes they take 120 seconds to jot, sometimes an hour to write, sometimes years to finish, yet I can never completely understand a single poemette.

- Written in mere seconds, a poemette is born into a slowly maturing child; whenever I reread my own, he needs more guidance, pruning, allegorical fine-tuning.

- In my mind, the pen gets in the way. Poetry is really, for me, finding the shortest possible distance from my heart to the reader.

Acknowledgements

With unfathomable gratitude, *#25wtT* is dedicated to the many friends and apparitions, seen and unseen, from across the world and those placeless places, who inspired, encouraged, and quite simply comprise the substance of so much that I've written. I'd especially like to thank my family—children and parents—for much more than your support, but for your love and tolerance over all these decades as I often drifted into aloof and reflective states. *Writing is not a talent. It's an affliction,* and it either leaves the author lonely, his family and friends distressed, or, on those more fortunate occasions, leaves him surrounded by the most amazing and understanding people. Finally, I am grateful to the One and the countless steps that have been taken along my life's path toward divine provenance.

1

Divine Inkling

We were given but a divine inkling
of what lies beyond mystery,
so that our minds might imagine
what only our hearts know for sure.

2

Mind Is Lumber

I climbed the highest tree
within the forest of my mind
only to look down
to find my heart at its base,
holding an axe.

3

Who Is Poet?

Some of us
simply write the poems
we hear in the hearts of others.
So one must ask
who is poet
and who is listener?

4

My Own Reflection

As apparent as I am to others,
I end up discovering what even I cannot see
when I find my own reflection
hidden within You.

5

Shadow Company

Enlighten our heart's voice
before we speak the darkness
of our minds,
for it is we who keep our shadow company,
not our shadow us.

6

Poems Lost at Sea

Love takes life.
Pain—respite.
Death—life's poetry.
When troubled
it's You I see,
a heart in a lighthouse
for a poem lost at sea.

7

I Hear Thunder

Your heart beats like mine.
Your exhalation sounds like mine.
Wounds and mountains between us,
We've storms to cross.
At the window, I hear thunder.

8

On Beloveds

There are pearls in you,
So I'll slip without splash
Into the pools between your lashes,
For the eyes have depths
Only lovers can dive.

9

Who You Are Is Everything

Who you are
Is whom you look out from.
Everything is *you* as *you* see it.
The world's a candle,
Your gaze stirring its steadiness.

10

The War on Errorism

They've nothing to live for.
They were dead before they died.
They wanted to make a difference
Between two principles,
Neither of which they understood.

11

Lost in Translation

The heart's path to the
writing hand
and speaking lips
is fraught with struggle
between ego and intellect.
Love's message becomes
a negotiation between them.

12

You Are Predator and Prey

Your true purpose
has been seen
by the hawk eyes
of a predator heart.
Listen for the wind
of diving wings—
you're your own prey.

13

You Can When You Can't

There are love's lessons
even when our candle is doused,
no flame to offer
and wick blackened.
Study the gaze of love
looking at you.

14

Love in the Balance

We desire love for hearts
like deserts thirst for rain.
Unquenched, we love most.
Fulfilled, we drown.
I'll risk my life to
know the difference.

15

Signs of the Wayfarer

God lays a joyful path before the
feet of the wayfaring hearts.
You can tell who they are
by the thinning soles of their shoes.

16

The Teacher Who Knows You

When we seek to know everything,
everyone looks like a divine murshid.
When we seek to know nothing,
we become the *murid* of the Divine.

17

The Phoenix

Full moon waning in
a waxing blue sky
before a blazing white sun—
so goes the soul.
Love burns to cinders
before a phoenix rises.

18

The Gambler

Every great poet is a lonely gambler
with an excess of income
in his swollen heart
and a wagering pen
on an endless losing streak.

19

Seeing with the Heart

Nothing can be more truthful
than beholding with the heart
that which cannot be seen with the eyes.
It is God's indescribable
light streaming through.

20

Earth beneath Feet

I'd compare myself
to the earth beneath his feet,
so that wherever Shams Tabrizi wanders,
I remain in his company—
such a friend is he!

21

Thunder Distantly

Should a storm rage within,
I'll stand at the windows of your soul,
watch the lightening in your eyes
and listen to you
thunder distantly.

22

Trifling Lips

Love flies on the voice of the wind
through wings.
Banter is a trifling gust past lips
raising a fading voice
to a wanting ear.

25

Reality of Truth—Truth of Reality

Reality isn't so apparent.
Its *absence* of internal truth
inspires the seeker to fill this *void*
with meaning sought through
poetry, beauty, romance, and esotericism.

26

Illuminusions

The illusion of love
is a manifestation withheld by God.
Those we love cannot darken our lives,
for truth's reflection illuminates them
from beyond death.

27

Curiosity Ushers in Reason

She walked out barefoot
into the snow,
her marveled curiosity
taking steps just ahead of reason.
In doing so,
she deciphered the secret
to self-discovery.

28

World on My Tongue

A snowflake fell on my tongue,
filling my mouth with the world.
The universe is a crystal ornament
hung by the soul in the heart.

29

One Last Gaze

I took one last gaze
As her flames found respite.
I, beside the warmth of her sun,
Stood at the cold edge of my night.

30

He Is, Therefore I Am

I didn't think *I* was possible
until I saw myself in my son.
Now, with certainty I see,
I am as He is—
in everyone.

31

A Bridge between Them

Words are neither of the heart
nor the mind
but a bridge between them.
Silence, above speech,
spans rivers of truth
on our way home.

32

The Key Is Locked in Its Vault

The key unlocking the realm of purpose
is hidden from thought.
Behold with love in your heart
all that the mind seeks through your eyes.

33

An Army of Loners

Those who walk the path of destruction
among an army of thousands
are more alone than one
who walks the path of peace by himself.

34

Of Conquest and Surrender

My pond, His ocean.
I'm adrift in her devotion,
seeking beyond earthly measure
not the conquest of her vision
but the silence in her surrender.

35

The Necklace Maker

What you seek
is a pearl in a shell
that must be broken open
with the blade of knowledge,
polished with love,
strung with prayer.

36

Lion's Dreams

What gives the lion his strength
is the softness of his dreams.
Within you, he discloses
the ferocity to remain still
in gentle, wide wonder.

37

Combustible Lovers

The lover is highly combustible.
As he becomes perfect,
he hears the strike of the Beloved's match
and rejoins the dance of the consummate flame.

38

Tears that Bond Us

All tears taste the same.
The deceased sit at the same table
as we feast on the sadness of memories.
My children's mother, your brother.

39

Eternity Unraveled

Why toil for years unraveling something
that took an eternity to tangle?
Submit your understanding
to the happening of now
versus the undoing of *then*.

40

Reassembling

What the mind shreds
the heart keeps whole.
The mind, the house,
the heart, the home within—
delicate duality.
Perfect poetry is reassembled,
not heard.

41

Perpetuity of Illusion

Cut loose from the reed bed,
we drift on serene waters,
holding the world's trickery in reverence,
for even illusion
wrought with *sincerity*
enjoys perpetuity.

42

The Tack of Our Path

'Tis not the wind
but its direction
filling the sail
along our journey.
A straight path
may change in its tack
but not our destination.

43

The Lovers Inhale

Men's hearts are still ships,
slack sails awaiting the wind of a lover,
a breeze inhaled, for to cross oceans
to find the Beloved exhaling.

44

The Cane

Pain is a broken man's staff,
entering his heart
as love flies from his hand
holding him up until love lands
in his heart again.

45

Out to Sea

Ocean waves curl
and fade on these shores
My true love is the persistent tide
delivering hope,
she whispers, notes,
"Beloved, return to my side."

46

The Lover's Whisper

I've discovered that God whispers
among those who proudly proclaim love.
The latter takes us for love's fool,
but I take the Whisperer as Lover.

47

Sojourners' Exchange

Those who give
travel within the deep hulls of the *given*,
building a seaworthy vessel.
The way your ship lists
is that of another's cargo.

48

None, but One

Faint attar at dawn,
quietly, sinuously,
slowly, by morning
she stirs the fashioner of winds.
Being a feather,
whenever Layla's close,
Majnun takes flight again.

49

The Pain of the Thorn

The pain of the thorn
pressed through the skin
is where the blood red rose
gets it color from and
where fragrance manifests
its poignant message.

50

Everything Is Everywhere

We occupy different parts of the earth
but share the same sky.
Look up. Everything is there—
boundless pastures of starlit imagination
roaming in halcyon.

51

Surrender of Vision

I am always amazed
at how far your eyes can see.
It is not the conquest of your vision,
but its surrender to the unseeable.

52

The Poet's Flame

God is poet, not outshone.
Covet not the light your own
lest out it goes.
Submit—'tis only His,
and your flame
the brighter glows.

53

Implements of Prayer

I prayed with eloquent mouth
and was left mute
I prayed with keen eyes
and was blinded
I prayed with an empty heart.
I'm fulfilled.

54

The Hearts of Children

The only species to not evolve
is the child within a human.
Save the world with the minds of adults
and the hearts of children.

55

Preempted by Idleness

In my quest to understand the world,
I'm continually preempted
by my own thought
of what, in the meantime,
I am to do *in* it.

56

Rose of Honesty

When I hand you the rose of honesty,
beware the thorns.
I've pricked my fingers many times
carrying it around for only me to see.

57

Love, the Racehorse

Love is like a racehorse
running wild
She doesn't know or care
whether she's won or lost,
only the exhilaration
of having run the race.

58

Another's Hope

I'd rather risk failure and sadness
navigating the promise
of my own uncertainty
than be enraptured
by the illusion of hope
cast by another's certainty.

59

Skin of Lips

The phone rings,
And you seem only feet away.
Oh, if that were true,
Only the thin skin of our lips
Would keep us apart.

60

Handholds of Youth

Hang on to our moments of youth.
They're the trusted handholds
and firm footing
for many slippery slopes
as we cross into our later years.

61

Seal of Trust

The seal of trust
marks the gates of love.
Even when love has closed its doors
between two people,
trust remains emblazoned
upon them both.

62

Forgetting to Remember

I really don't mind forgetting the *right* places I put things
as much as I do having to remember
the *wrong* places I left them.

63

Stirring the Depths

You, a fathomless pool of silver water,
I stir your surface
with the pass of a gentle hand,
and your depths glisten before my eyes.

64

Instruments of Self-Observation

I have learned in life
sometimes truth—even our own—
is largely a function of
how well we calibrate and hone
the instruments of self-observation.

65

Loud Birds

Better silent
with the grace of a hummingbird
in a flowerpot
than parroting the proclamations of a magpie
perched atop the branch of an evergreen.

66

The Pause

What fails to express meaning,
is best understood in the next pure pause
between a perfect feeling
and a word desperately wanting
to explain it.

67

Path beneath Our Feet

Infinite paths
all cross briefly at one point.
'Tis best that each encounter count,
each breath last,
and that all paths persevere
beneath one's feet.

68

Absence Desires Us

The density of absence
exceeds that which is absent,
creating its own gravitational pull,
so we fall toward the center
as if *it* desires *us*.

69

Invention and Art

When the beauty of man's invention
exceeds its utility,
and when eyes can see
the aesthetics of creative process
before its object,
then art evolves.

70

Each Word a Metaphor

Words are metaphors, divine ideas
whose quality is approximated
through language.
True truth to which each points
is unutterable, unfathomable—inaudible echoes
caressing the heart.

71

The Measure of I

The pain of the thorn
is where the rose receives its color,
where fragrance
manifests its message,
but the measure of *I*
is ultimately hidden.

72

One Divine Channel

Amidst all this plurality
is a deeply personal
and singular experience.
Yet, the plentitude of poetry
runs like many rivers—wild
within a single divine channel.

73

Wisdom Says Nothing

When the mind speaks,
wisdom puts a finger to its lips
and says, "Hush."
Let us not be interrupted
by the constant quest for order.

74

The Ocean in Your Tears

Does not even the smallest tear
taste the same as a vast ocean?
Yet, is not the ocean
still a place
to empty your sorrows?

75

Where is Shams Tabrizi?

What you seek with the mind
ends with the heart.
For Shams,
the bottom of a lost well
differs little
from the heights of halcyon.

76

Pawns of Pronouns

We are the pawns of pronouns.
In "I love you,"
who is "I" and who is "you"
when love is the bridge
between blurred identities?

77

The Thirsty Pauper's Pen

You're the scribe of your soul.
A wealthy writer wields a pauper's pen.
Only parched thirst
can drink from the unfathomable inkwell
of the divine.

78

The Door to Her Heart

Men wear themselves out
trying to enter a woman
who will never reveal
the real door to her heart,
no matter how naked she gets.

79

My Poverty Is My Pride

The poverty of the heart
empathizes with the poor,
sharing what little it has,
and the less we have,
the more valuable what's given becomes.

80

Seek What You Have

I've only sought one thing,
and there is no other,
so how can I be poor,
when choosing one among one
and receiving it all?

81

Poetic Ingredients

You read My poems
as I remembered you,
and you taste something
faintly palatable on the tongue—
but you will never know
the Poets ingredients.

82

The Color of Your Cloak

By cloak's color,
each sect declares itself
closest to God.
But the spiritual truth
of the individual
reigns over the religious illusion
of the masses.

83

Hearts in Flames

Winter of my melting,
I ran past the fallen leaves,
crisp pages mired by frost
in the frozen earth.
But my heart was in flames.

84

Leave a Fulfilling Stone

I've picked up many stones
etched with words of encouragement,
but none so fulfilling
as those I've scribed
and left behind for others to read.

85

Innocent Innovators

As age smothers the innocent innovator,
we often protect what's within
by never letting it out.
Then one day
we no longer remember our dreams.

86

Humble Understanding

I'm humble in two ways:
One is not presuming I understand enough.
The other is never telling anyone
I understand as much as I do.

87

Unable to Sway Any Longer

Throughout the progression toward adulthood,
the surface of the child
is wounded and scarred,
like tree bark around the sapling, impenetrable
but unable to sway.

88

God's Plan: One for All

You ask for glimpses of God's plan for you.
You fail to understand
that God plans at all for another
is his plan for you.

89

The Value of Injury

Do not purge an experience
that has let you down
in order to heal.
There is no regeneration of spirit
when the injury is discounted.

90

Color within the Lines

Creativity uncloaks passion
otherwise imprisoned
by the broad black lines
in our coloring books
with the grown-up instruction,
"Shush now, and color within the lines."

91

Life Half Empty, Half Full

Time spent regretting yesterday
is balanced by
a longing to change tomorrow.
Life is half fulfilled
between what just happened
and what will happen next.

92

The Question to Your Answer

The answer's the wind
that fills a questioning sail.
Onward over the crests we go,
urging us to reach our destination
long before we arrive.

93

The Beginning Again

I'm a thimble afloat in a sea of wisdom,
riding low in the water,
waiting for rain
that I might sink
into my beginning again.

95

Shared Crisis, Shared Peace

If the multitudes can perish
individually in crisis,
then we can coexist
as one in peace.
There are no chosen people,
just people who choose.

94

Mind Asks about the Heart

What's to understand
if we cannot take truth on faith
into our heart to feel.
Questions by the mind about the heart
always remain unanswered.

96

Weak Foundations

Never suffer those
who deftly climb the shoulders of idiots
to vehemently proclaim their wisdom.
The summit of reality
eventually weathers back
to true foundation.

97

Well-Versed Fools

A wise man well versed
in the ways of a fool
is recognized by the foolishness of his words
before the wisdom of his meaning.

98

Bound to Collide

What you take deeply within you
surrounds you from the inside,
presses your back up against a world
that cannot avoid the collision fast enough.

99

A Heart Doesn't Wait

The day that waits too long
reminds us
that time offers more of a promise
than a denial.
Surely a heart waits not for time.

100

Don't Wake Up

Gently whirl about.
Wake not this sleeping muse
Else I'll disappear in night-stream.
Where do I exist?
In other worlds
Or here within her dreams?

101

Sans Word

Sans a single word
printed from the scribed voice of mystic poets,
the unwritten meaning of their poetry
would flow beyond an eternity of bookshelves.

102

A Thousand Suns

Gaze silently with a humble heart,
for one quiet candle
can consume a thousand suns
and be blown out
by a single pair of lips.

103

Intention (Niyat)

Intention is like a pebble in a shoe.
It can change the course of mankind
with little more than a minor discomfort
in our step.

104

Teaspoons of Light

I offer teaspoons of light
to feed the darkness,
yet it growls with hunger.
Nothing craves light
like a shadow
wanting to show its secret.

105

Share Threshold

Seek nothing and leave everything.
Realms we enter and realms we exit
share the same threshold.
We are the door—and both sides of it.

106

Shortsighted Youth

We were young and tormented
by the significance of our recent past,
because at such an age
we'd never fathomed
the rest of our lives.

107

A Moment

There is no room for judgment
or time for question in a moment.
If so, you are either too late or too soon.
Pause here.

108

Love's Understanding

Truth lies along the less-visited fringe
of the bizarre and logical,
and while it eludes man's rationalized definition,
it is not beyond love's complete understanding.

109

Inevitable Flow of Peace

Those who
surrender to the channel of peace
rather than divergent routes of conquest
are lost rivers far inland,
flowing quietly, ultimately
toward the ocean.

110

Retrospective on War

I'm certain in retrospect
that not one loss of a single life in any war
effected a change
that wasn't in some way
deeply regretted.

111

Journey's End

Out to the continent's edge, expecting
answers by journey's end,
we stand on wave-washed driftwood, perplexed
as the mind lets go where the heart begins.

112

Men Split in Two

My mind fought for purchase
upon a piece of driftwood, while my heart
surrendered to the ocean.
Men split in two
when standing before such starkness.

113

Find You

I wish to know who You are
And to not possess You,
To find You
Over and over again,
Especially when I'm no longer looking.

114

Discomfort with Your Direction

Your intention is a pebble within a shoe.
It can change the course of life
with little more
than a minor discomfort beneath your step.

115

Message to Artist Chris Trapper

Humans should be humbled
by the miraculous gift of song,
We are guided by nature to compose
where oft led by our egos to recite.

116

Bad Poetic Decisions

A writer secretly wants
to make bad decisions
and ache with the pains
of poetic purpose.
Our regretted mistakes offer course corrections
along the path.

117

Unlearning

Enlightened states
for the reparation of humanity
are achieved by *unlearning* layers of opacity.
Divided over future states,
we share the same past and present.

118

The Divine Feminine

Conversation blazes many trails
given the spectrum of masculinity
but only navigates
through the power to surrender
to the inarguable forces
of the divine feminine.

119

The Battle of Smiling

A smile is more recognizable
through tears than laughter.
The war between the teeth and the lips
is decided by
a smile's submission to joy.

120

Darkness in Search of Light

We cannot benefit others *ever*
if not ourselves *always*.
'Tis futile looking for colors in others' lives
when the light of our own is off.

121

A Breeze beyond Seasons

Love's a breeze stirring a million leaves,
each believing itself in love
with its rustling companions,
yet they let go of each other in autumn.

122

Lumps of Clay

While each lump of clay on a potter's wheel
may seem the same,
their hidden potential to be something else
is what truly distinguishes them.

123

The Grand Potter

Lovers thrown as clay
onto the Grand Potter's wheel,
in love with and seen by the Unseen,
joyful with what they are
and will become.

124

Never Complete

Love is never complete
as there's never been a dusk so beautiful
that the earth and sun would conspire
to not show us another day.

125

God's Warrior

God took a tiny dagger from one hand
and put a sword in the other.
This is how He both saves and takes a life.

126

Secrets Withheld

The illusion of love for another
is a manifestation of a secret
withheld from us by God.
Loving within darkness
sees Truth's reflection
beyond death.

127

Tough as Tree Bark

My grandfather's skin
was tough as tree bark.
He only died on the outside,
but inside he was still a tree,
a big, wise tree.

128

Ancient Press

Poetry is the ancient press
for the records of humanity—
the literary crypt keeper
dragging its demons and fairies
from open graves to restful cemetery.

129

Forgetting upon My Death

While not living the way we'd hoped,
we've the right to hope
that what failed
upon our death dies too,
departing the memory of others.

130

Journalists of Death

As a journalist of death,
through the lens of my camera
I've seen the persistence of life
in the faces of children
who've never lived.

131

Terrorism

Love fills a canyon wide.
Evil needs but a thin crack to seep inside,
consuming a heart, thirsting life
in those dead before they died.

132

True Art

A true artist can look at a block of marble
and know the true form within it
before the chisel is ever set and struck.

133

Living Books

Books have ghostly hands.
From the tomb
of bookshelves they hear me
and tug pleadingly on the fabric of my heart
as I walk by.

134

Time the Redeemer

But a second for each stirring word within,
I'd redeem them all for years,
so I might have eternity to bask
in their unspoken meaning.

135

Patterns of One

Ptolemy and I stared into a clear dark night.
He asked, "What do you see?"
"Stars," I said, "and you?"
He smiled. "I see constellations."

136

Patterns of One (Part Two)

We both saw God—
she found it in patterns,
I in the randomness—
yet God is as the darkness
without which stars would not shine.

137

Everything Is Becoming

Sadness is the stark realization
that everything must run out.
Happiness is knowing that running out
is just everything else
in the process of becoming.

138

Return, Try Again

I'm just one wave in an ocean
that tumbles and fades on your shores.
The tide of true love retrieves me,
imploring,
"Return. Try again."

139

Acuity of a Heart

Longing for love reminds us
that nothing of divine meaning
is ever truly lost
to anything other
than the visual acuity of an unobservant heart.

140

Unseen Signs

Unseen signs never give up
their quest for being seen.
With a slight tilt of the head,
the heart's light changes,
and so does everything.

141

Greater than I Can Carry

I've loved in ways
that have become gifts
greater than I can carry—
oh, the importance of knowing
how to offload
this burden to others.

142

The Drunkard's Heart

This intoxication does not arise
from the wine in the bottle,
but rather from the ripened heart of the drunkard
before the sober grape ferments.

143

Let Go of the Rope

Love surrounds those
who surround others with love.
Circumscribe yourself, for
hatred is fear tied to a soul. 'Tis
love lets go of the rope.

144

Waiting on a Breeze

Being moved gently
by words of love
is an ember of hope in a darkened hearth,
waiting for a breeze
to raze the flame again.

145

Pause Tenderly

These moments become the underpinnings
of a forever that is behind us.
Pause tenderly in this moment,
and you'll discover love stands due before you.

146

Human Gem

The human being is a faceted gem
that cannot contain its true light.
Those who love genuinely and divinely
emanate their clarity, color, and cut.

147

Less Hurts the Most

There's often less pain over all that's lost
than there is for not at least once having
some of what would otherwise never be found.

148

Fathers beyond Places

Even fathers passing beyond earthly limits
carry the persistent memory of their children—
this flame of paternal love, legendary,
recast by the light of God.

149

Torchbearers

The torch you carry
does not provide the light
with which you seek your beloved,
but rather is that by which the Beloved finds you.

150

Your Light Everywhere

If you keep your love glowing,
fueled through your self-awareness,
your light will become the reflected glint
within the eyes of another who sees you.

151

My Alma Mater

In a belletristic sense,
every moment of life
is the scenic route home,
every poem is a homecoming,
and my heart is my alma mater.

152

Edge of Disbelief

In rivers of endless possibilities,
you're quenched by one curling eddy of illusion,
while currents of truth
disappear like myths over the edge of disbelief.

153

Warriors of the Mind and Heart

Fateful, besieged tellurian
seeking whence his end began.
A northern throne for
a southern heart
thereupon ascends, proclaims,
"I've come to free this writing hand."

154

Words in an Hourglass

Damned words.
Pouring through me like
grains of sand
from the womb of the writer's mind
to the readers heart,
and the hourglass
turns again.

155

Dare to Thrive

Dare to thrive
like dew clinging to threads of spider silk;
Sliding down moment by moment,
whenever the breath of our prey
quivers the chord.

156

The Realm of Nothingness

Fret not
on this plane of earthly existence,
for all you've loved
within all that seems lost
remains *as is* in the realm
of nothingness.

157

Not What, but That

It's not *what*, but *that* you do.
Loving *that* you're doing something,
is more gratifying
than only loving what you do
after you've done it.

158

The Unheard Ripples

One teardrop released into Your silent pond
whispers back a thousand secrets
that can only be heard by those
with the patience of a mountain.

159

Sufis

Careening seekers of divine rapture
hold their heads as cups,
pouring wine from their hearts.
"Besotted lovers, painters, scholars, poets!
Only the lost are found."

160

Misperception of Fear

Fear is the misperception
that all we can ever have
is all we can hold today,
exceeding all we might discover
in moments to come.

161

Fear and Love Differ by One Breath

Fear and love
are two reflections of one soul
within the same mirror.
Whichever has the breath to fog the glass
is the truth—
breath.

162

The Sextant of the Soul

The sextant of the soul navigates these stars,
yet it takes but a gentle turn of the helm
to spin the heavens around the heart.

163

Happiness

Happiness heeds not the distinction
between where we're heading
and whence we came,
thus existing in the moment
with an insignificant capacity to hold fear.

164

Dubious Endeavors

I've taken to dubious endeavors
with the best intentions at stake,
more receptive to the unknown possibilities
than the certitude of the choices
I'd make.

165

The Devil's Duality

The struggle of being human
is maintaining awareness of inner self
while passing through the nexus of the devil's duality,
that being rigidity and chaos.

166

Path of Nondescription

No easy route—
among those of least resistance,
many ways to walk this path,
many paths to take this walk
beyond description, time, and distance.

167

Self

You've no greater value than that unto yourself.
Create where it is you choose to go,
and your path will appear for all that follows.

168

All Roads End

All roads chosen
share a single end.
No matter its terrain
or whose roads blend,
'tis not the route,
but how each step is taken.

169

Too Busy Listening

One long evening a friend asked frustratedly,
"Are you listening to anything I'm saying?"
"Sorry, no," I answered.
"I'm busy listening to what I hear."

170

Move or Be Moved

It is best to be a strand of force
in the trestle of braided motion
than an object that can be simply moved by others.

171

Creating Resistance

We create what we resist.
Resistance comes with the symptom
of indirectly studying and ideologically manifesting
what it is we previously only suspected we'd feared.

172

Symphony of Life

Our lives, each of us,
are perfectly tuned instruments,
objects of intrigue in our stillness, yet
exquisitely beautiful
when played within the symphony of life.

173

Aging Instruments

In departing life's orchestra,
my strings may snap and wood warp,
but my music is indelible.
I am the finale of my own beautiful sound.

174

Lost and Found

"Your soul is a diamond's shine,"
said the smiling sage,
"abandoned by birth,
lost in the dunes,
and found
again in the sands by age."

175

An End to My Means

The failure to find order in my life
is evidence that I'm seeking the means with my mind
rather than the ends with my heart.

176

To Die Anew

The rose endures its falling petals,
reuniting with the soil
from which it grows anew.
Were I not to die,
what use is this life?

177

Secrets in the Shadows

Within the darkness
a secret passage lies.
We who keep our stirred hearts still,
from these shadows truth will spill,
And there our purposes rise.

178

Content sans Container

I'm content
sans container,
A sinner when I do right,
a saint when wrong,
the feeling you're not alone
and a reminder that you are.

179

World out of Tune

The world is a chorus out of key.
And just then, a beautiful voice
with rising volume
inspires harmony among others,
finishing the grand symphony.

180

Shadows' Spotlight

Cast light on fear.
You'll find it's simply love
in the shadows of the unknown.
Turn this light on ourselves and
our shadows fall away.

181

Tattered Robes

We clothe ourselves in a shared and colorful fabric
woven in promise with another.
If either violates that integrity,
we both suffer in tattered robes.

182

Intersections

I pause to reflect at our paths' intersections.
In these moments
whence we came or where we go
is but the same infinitely small point.

183

The Friend

I remember the sound of your voice
and the timeless meaning of your words.
They are like two old friends
embracing sweetly in the heart!

184

Gnosis Unwritten

It's not writing that brings me closer to God,
but moments when beauty lures me from the pen,
like ink from the vial
spilling free.

185

Deluded Authors

Waiting patiently
until the hand of God takes our pens
and writes us onto His parchment.
How vain to believe
we are the true authors.

186

Thread of Truth

Love is a string tied around the finger.
All is fragile but the knot.
'Tis the heart that binds
threadbare souls
behind the Beloved's frock.

187

The Neyzen's Lips

How can the ney flute remain silent
when the wild cane was cut
to kiss the neyzen's lips
and deliver sweet breath
before empty ears?

188

The Shell

Time's relentless assault on the body
within which awaits a seed
cracked and open, deep in the soil,
from this heart springs a spirit, freed.

189

Khamoshiyan Company

The empty space next to me
is a place of immortality—
a revelation
that the mystery of good company arrives
where words cannot be found.

190

Majnun

Majnun still glows
after the song of the candle's flame
goes out.
He'll sing no more,
while his beloved
seeks him again
through their silence.

191

What Remains

The intricacy of disclosure
unfolds so slowly
like a rose opening.
I find there is even as much
beauty in what has yet to blossom.

192

Blind Poet

On a most cathartic trip to the sea,
I found so much darkness in light.
I wrote clearly
until I just couldn't see anymore.

193

How Nature Reaches In

Nothing comes closer to capturing
such rich and varied hues in nature
than our own eyes,
stretching memories across our hearts
like colors on canvas.

194

Brevity

I found endless stories through my own brevity.
I saw one leaf fall and remembered a forest.
I took one breath, and the world sighed.

195

18:78

Seek naught but silently
that path beneath your feet,
for all will be explained
by the most trusted companion
who rises higher with each step.

196

Hatred

Hatred doesn't have a target.
It *is* the target.
It's preyed upon by fear
and will don anything or anyone
as its disguise for hiding.

197

We Speak Often

We are oceans, eons,
and one thousand circumstances apart.
Yet, I speak with You often,
depending on how I listen,
depending on what I hear.

198

Creative Intercession

Creative inspiration finds
entrances to your heart,
especially when your time is scant.
Crawl into these spaces hidden from time,
and manifest its artful essence.

199

Hidden

There is a peaceful calm
in the burning desire to know oneself.
I'd not know what to do
were I not hidden from my view.

200

What Comes Next

There's no distinguishing the path,
deeds, or intentions
in a dying man's last breath.
Rather, each shares in the same mystery
of what comes next.

201

The Ferry Ticket

Real love is the last ticket to anywhere—
the water, the ferryboat, the captain,
the "bon voyage,"
but most of all
the continents it spans.

202

What's More Perfect

There is something beyond wisdom.
Perhaps the seed was always more perfect
than the tree that grew
from its tiny scar etched beneath the dirt.

203

Word Flirtations

Light streaks the universe
Looking for something to fall upon.
Words mark the vain wandering
of a mind tormented by flirtations
of a speechless heart.

204

Flames Rejoined

We are kindled by our own inspiration
and burn toward the light of a single flame,
but as waning embers,
there's only darkness between us.

205

I See Your Silence

Some sounds I hear
through your silence.
You're listening,
And I am waiting
Until you echo.
Then you see my point,
And I hear music.

206

Dull Hearts

Deliver unto the people a message.
We spun out from a still,
timeless, and infinitely small center.
We honed our intellect
and dulled our hearts.

207

Love Ripens on a Dying Vine

Of all the men and women of beauty I've loved,
none rivals that love which I leave alone
to ripen as it passes into seasons.

Coming Soon

#15wtT

Within the soul of the beloved reader
is a patient universe waiting to be written.

There are no limits
to discovering something within others
if they see themselves as limitless.

I beseech destiny for answers
while destiny beseeches me
to stop asking so many questions.

What use is my bright lantern
if I fear the shadows
in those I'll encounter?

Could it be
that the altar of happiness
is built on the ruins of sorrow?

This intoxication isn't in the grape or the wine,
but pre-eternally in the drunkard's heart.

I'd been held captive by love for another,
until love of wisdom set her free.

In seeking to know someone,
we begin with what we seek to observe
within ourselves.

Wherever we are heading
is kindly guided by the certainty
of where we are now.

About the Author

Skip Maselli lives in northern Virginia, but resides somewhere between earth and heaven. Raised in the rural areas of southern New Jersey, far from the turnpike, he left for more remote parts of the earth, ending up in the most amazing places, from Korea to Europe, from Australia and the Pacific Rim to Turkey and southwest Asia, and points in between. Skip has been writing and reciting his poetry, prose, quips, and vignettes since he was 11 years old. The genre of his writing delves into various ontological explorations of mysticism, divine and human love, spiritual awakening, and socio-cultural and interpersonal musings. Indeed, you might find Sufi undertones in his writing. His next book, "A Sparrow Who Ate the Universe" is expected to be out in the spring of 2016.

Skip received his bachelor's degree from Dickinson College with a focus in geology and philosophy, a combination that at the time made perfect sense. After receiving his master's in civil and environmental engineering from the University of Wisconsin Skip served in the military, which provided him yet another view of the world. As an offset to his current career in business development for a large corporation he remains an impassioned reader, thinker, and deep listener. Many of his views have been shaped as a competitive swimmer and triathlete and spiritual explorationist. He is still called "Daddy" by his highly creative and gifted daughter Camerin, fifteen, and her wisely inquisitive brother, Aidan, twelve who lost their mother three years ago. His work and play reflect a life of inward travels, long drives, short phrases, small disappointments, big lessons – all flavored by serendipity, loving partnerships, and God-sent children and friends.

Printed in the United States
By Bookmasters